Escaping the Invasion

A Mother's Account of the Invasion of Kuwait

Huda M. Al-Medlej

Al Medlej, Huda.

Escaping the invasion : a mother's account of the invasion of Kuwait / Huda M. Al-Medlej.

Kuwait : The Author, 2013.

p.   ;   cm.

ISBN: 978-99966-0-299-3

Depository No. 131/2013

      1. Oraq-Kuwait crisis, 1990-1991.
      2. Persian Gulf War, 1991-Miscellanea. I. Title.

NLK   DS79.72   956.70442   tlc00038902

Copyright © 2011 By Huda Al-Medlej
All Rights Reserved.

ISBN-10: 1456553240

ISBN-13: 9781456553241

My son Abdullah

Dedication

To my beloved children Abdullah, Hamad, Shaha, and Mohammed Al-Khamees , here is a little adventurous story to tell your children!

To my source of love, strength and hope, Ahmed my best friend and husband , thank you for the infinitive support.

HUDA M. AL-MEDLEJ

Foreword

By Abdullah

My name is Abdullah. I'm seventeen years old now, but when this true story took place, I was only seven months old!

My mother wrote this book when she sensed that I was ready to hear what once happened to our family. She decided to take me back years ago to tell me about the biggest tragedy that ever happened to our beloved country.

She wanted to tell me about what our family went through when Kuwait was invaded by Iraq .So every night she started telling me the story.

Her face would lite up with exhilaration and pride when she recalled how I survived a real war. Many nights, my mother used to sit beside my bed and recite to me how tough I'd been as a little boy. I used to like hearing what had happened to me. She sat night after night reciting the ordeal that our family had experienced.

Listening to her made me a stronger boy. I believe that if I survived what we went through, I can tackle any hardship in my life.

Every night I would jump in my bed, waiting to hear more of her astounding story.

Now, my mother has turned this family story into a book for all the children of the world to learn about what we went through.

Introduction

My name is Huda and I wrote this story for my children and all the children of the world who hadn't been born yet, when one small country called Kuwait was completely conquered in one day by a neighboring country called Iraq.

Our whole country was invaded for seven long months. The invasion concluded with the biggest war of the twentieth century: Desert Storm.

Desert Storm gave freedom to almost one million Kuwaitis who were either under siege in their own country or forced to leave and go to other countries. Many Kuwaitis were killed or captured. There were 605 prisoners who were taken to the Iraqi jails throughout the whole seven months.

Although the number of captives may seem rather small, this actually amounted to nearly 0.1 percent of the total Kuwaiti population. This means that for every one thousand Kuwaiti, one was being held as a POW (according to the National Committee of Missing & Prisoners of War-Kuwait).

I am glad the invasion came to an end, but the stories remain and must be shared. I wrote this story with my children in mind and my beloved country in my heart. By now it has been almost twenty years since the invasion, but my memories are still sharp and the pain is still raw.

This story may relate to many people in the world. It's the typical evil and good fairytale. It meant to continuously remind you to never give up on holding hopes to regain your taken right of living . And that no bigger power can deprive you of what you love.

Kuwaiti POWs

Iraqi troops in Kuwait streets

Chapter One

A Knock on the Door

Knock knock!

"Wake up! Iraq has invaded Kuwait!"

Those were the first words I heard on that bright and sunny morning of August 2, 1990. It was a "black Thursday" that no Kuwaiti will ever forget.

"It must be a joke or some kind of false news report," I first thought. "Why is my mother-in-law waking us up this early on the weekend to say this?"

I turned over in my warm bed, preparing for deeper sleep as my husband Ahmed went out of the room to check. When he came back ten minutes later, there was a look on his face that I had never encountered in our four years of marriage.

"Is that right?" I exclaimed with a sluggish voice and half-opened eyes, not expecting his response. He nodded gravely. I saw deep sorrow in his face and absolute shock at the same time.

Escaping the Invasion

Still in disbelief, I immediately jumped out of my bed, put on my robe, and went to the front door. I couldn't believe what I saw. On the horizon, dozens of army trucks filled with Iraqi soldiers descended upon the main street across from our house.

I was stunned. I felt my heart torn into pieces. It was the saddest and the darkest moment in my life.

Our house was located in the northern part of Kuwait City, toward the border of our neighboring Iraq. Iraq was ruled at that time by a dictator named Saddam Hussein. Hussein had secretly planned the invasion many years before. He wished to have our small country under his utter and complete control. He wanted power and mainly the oil, which Kuwait is famous for.

I dragged myself back to my room, thinking of my seven-month-old boy. He felt very warm and couldn't sleep the night before because of a fever.

"What is going to happen to him?" I thought. "Are we going to live to see him become a young man? What is going to happen to my beloved country?"

I pulled myself from under those heavy thoughts and started packing for a few days in case the situation got worse. I wanted to ensure my son's food supply in case we needed to go without. To be safe, I assumed the worst-case scenario and began putting cans of milk and baby food in his diaper bag.

I then hid my fine jewelry in a safe place.

Not knowing what would happen was the scariest feeling, especially once we heard that Iraqi troops were invading Kuwaiti homes.

On the radio, we heard scattered news of the Iraqi troops taking over main government buildings. In the early hours of the morning, and with the dimmest light of dawn, the Iraqis began their deadly mission by approaching Dasman the presidential palace.

The amir (prince), Sheik Jabber Al-Ahmed Al-Sabah, the head of the state, had miraculously escaped just before Iraqi paratroopers landed alongside the palace. Other troops on the ground attacked with tanks as they tried to surprise and capture the amir while he slept.

However, Crown Prince Sheik Saad Al-Abdullah Al-Sabah had sensed danger and insisted that the amir, who was refusing to flee, ride in his car to a safer location. A few moments after their car drove out of the gates, Iraqi troops flooded into the palace. Many Kuwaiti guards were killed while defending the famous royal palace.

The morning had just broken, and most people were sleeping at that time. They did not realize what was happening at the most vital place in Kuwait—the amir's residence! The guards weren't expecting to face the artillery of one of the toughest and biggest armies in the world at that time.

One of the men killed was the brave younger brother of our amir, Sheik Fahad Al-Ahmed Al-Sabah. He was a very ambitious and admirable man. He was unfortunately killed

Escaping the Invasion

while approaching the palace to take part in defending the amir. But a sniper shot him dead! He was left there injured for more than hour, bleeding in his car, until he died bravely in the line of duty.

His death and the deaths of all the other men weren't in vain. The head of the state, the great symbol of Kuwait, was saved from almost the perfect crime of the century. He was taken safely to a secure location outside the borders of Kuwait. There, he worked tirelessly to regain his stolen country.

Later on that day, the Kuwaiti officials managed to acquire a secret radio station. They used it to stay connected with the world and the Kuwaiti people. Our minister of defense came onto the radio station. With a hoarse and choked voice, he explained the difficult circumstances to the world. He called upon all countries for help.

Sheik Fahad Al Ahmed Al Sabah, the Amir's brother

Escaping the Invasion

For three long days, the whole world was in disbelief and only watched what happened in Kuwait without taking any action. The presidents of the all the countries of the world needed time to absorb and to assess the situation before taking sides. It was a bizarre situation. A country suddenly and entirely invading its little peaceful neighboring country.

My family and I managed to get through the first day. We sat numbly in one room all together, my husband, his elderly parents, his sister, our little boy, and me. There was much nervous anticipation. We were paralyzed by the news. Unable to function normally while our country was overtaken by a sudden brutal attack.

In the middle of that frightening and eerie time, the night slowly wrapping us with its insecurity, we all heard one big noise on the front door of our house. Then there was a continuous ringing of the doorbell. We all froze and looked to each other in panic.

Chapter Two

The Big Noise

We could only imagine what it would turn out to be. I held on tight to my son, refusing to open the door. Our fears increased with each ring of the bell.

I looked my husband in the eyes and whispered in a very stern voice to *not* open the door. Suddenly, we heard a hard knock on the side door, which was closer to the room where we were gathering. That shook us even more.

I started trembling. My husband wanted to see who it was, but he was reluctant to move towards the door to find out. The door was shaking from the unyielding knocking.

Ahmed finally went over to look through the front door's upper glass to see who was trying to get inside. As he approached the door, I pleaded, "Please, don't open it."

Disregarding my plea, he asked in a low voice, "Who is it?"

An unclear response came from outside. As my husband double-checked the answer, I saw his hand moving to the doorknob.

"That's it…this is the end," I thought as my heart beat heavily.

Ahmed opened the door. To our surprise and great relief, it was his older brother, a major in the Kuwaiti Air Force.

He and his wife had come to check on their parents. Relieved with joy, we hugged. Then they joined us in the room. My brother-in-law told us what had taken place throughout the day. He also told us about the tough fight between the Iraqi invaders and the surprised but stubborn Kuwaiti armed forces.

At the end of that long, terrible day, through the night and into the dawn, I could still hear scattered gunfire outside. It was a sound that, up until that day, I had never heard before.

In my bed, I closed my eyes.

Chapter Three

The Devastating Move

Morning came with a frightening blast. Slowly I peeked from my window to the east. I saw high clouds of heavy gray smoke in the sky. I could hear heavy gunshots and artillery blasts.

The invading Iraqi troops were positioned just behind our house in an open area. They were shooting at the Kuwaiti National Guard base, three miles away.

The horrifying scene unfolded before my eyes. We were in a war zone! It was difficult to envision myself in the midst of heavy weapon fire.

"Is it a nightmare?" I thought. "Am I in a dream?"

In another part of the country, the Iraqis took over the national television station. They announced disturbing news about the abduction of high Kuwaiti government officials.

They said that the Kuwaiti people must denounce their Kuwaiti identity and declare Iraq as their native country! The Iraqis expected Kuwaitis to comply without resistance. They expected us to give up our country in a matter of days!

Escaping the Invasion

Iraqis tanks in residential area

The following morning, because of the dangerous circumstances and for our safety, we made a devastating and difficult decision. We decided to leave our house and join our relatives in a safer area.

Abandoning our home, our belongings, and our memories was the toughest decision we had ever made. I remember looking in every corner of my blue carpeted room. It felt like an ocean with deep water, and I couldn't swim in. With tears in my eyes, I gazed at my son's white crib with his musical toys hanging above.

"Am I going to see it again?" I thought. "Will my son Abdullah ever sleep in it again?"

With a broken heart and trembling hands, I closed the door to my bedroom. I looked down, feeling depressed. I was unsure of what the future would bring.

We drove away in our gold Mercedes. It was around ten o'clock in the morning.

Driving in Kuwait City wasn't like before. The streets looked like a war zone. They were almost empty of people. There were cars dumped on the roadside, doors hanging open. Some buildings along the road were burnt black.

There were sweaty Iraqi soldiers all over the place, gazing fiercely at us. Their faces were gloomy, worn-out, and sun-tanned. They looked as if they had been under the sun for ages. There was no expression in their faces but emptiness and purposelessness.

It was a ten-minute ride to our relative's house in southern Kuwait City. The neighborhood, a quiet suburb, was a little bit safer than our home. Our home was closer to the fighting.

The house was already full with five other families. Parents and children of our extended family were all finding shelter in the large basement which remarkably fit us all. We all shared the space and transformed it into a whole big bedroom in the night and a living room in the daytime.

One week passed. The news concerning the Iraqi soldiers got worse. Food supplies were not coming to them from Iraq, so they began looting and stealing anything they could get their filthy hands on. They intruded into many Kuwaiti homes and stole food, valuables, television sets, furniture, electronics, and even cars. My father's house was one of these. Luckily no one was there.

Iraqi soldiers looting Kuwait

Chapter Four

Wiping Out a Country

In the process of what could be called an organized robbery, the soldiers did not care about the peace of the Kuwaiti families. We were helpless under the imposed authority of the Iraqis. They forcibly entered houses without permission. They would threaten fathers to kill their children if they wouldn't give them food, water, and other possessions.

Kuwaitis were under a lot of pressure. They couldn't defend their loved ones. They had no means to protect themselves. Men were terrified for the safety of their wives and children.

The situation got worse and worse. Stories circulated of young men being killed for no reason other than defending their properties. Some people were killed in front of their moms and dads. Some women were raped and brutally tortured.

The Iraqi soldiers, by the order of their high command, let loose the animals of the Kuwaiti Zoo. Then they used their cages as prisons for the men and women who dared to resist them, young and old alike.

Escaping the Invasion

Zoo prison

The Iraqis stole our whole country in front of our bare eyes. They demanded Kuwaitis denounce their identity and nationality and declare Iraq as their country. They expected Kuwaitis to adhere to this without resistance. But no one agreed.

Proudly, there was not even one single Kuwaiti who submitted to the will of the Iraqis. No one agreed to what the Iraqis had to offer as a reward if they would participate in the new government.

They also tried to bribe the citizens, in order to expose the methods of the Kuwaiti fierce resistance against the occupation. But no one accepted that either.

Al-Qurain house, a battle field

The Kuwaitis were even forced to change their cars' license plates to a new format that read "The Nineteenth District of Iraq."

People who refused would be taken to jail in Iraq, and their families would know nothing about them. Many families were separated. A total of 605 hostages, including men, women, and children, were taken and later brutally killed.

Saddam Hussein wanted to erase Kuwait from the world map! Could such a thing happen? The whole world witnessed the dictator's awful treatment towards the peaceful little state of Kuwait.

Stay or leave

Chapter Five

Stay or Leave?

After a week, the situation did not improve. My husband tried to convince his father and his older brother to leave the country. He hoped we could escape before harm came to us all. Many members of the family refused the idea of leaving Kuwait. Others were unable to make a decision.

Then we got a phone call from my uncle. He was the chief commander of the Marines in the Saudi Arabian Navy. He urged us to leave as soon as we could. He told us, "A war might erupt to kick the Iraqis out of Kuwait."

The United Nations along with the United States of America were standing on the side of Kuwait. The amir succeeded in rallying our allies around the world to give us their support. The United Nations gave Saddam Hussein a period of time to leave Kuwait. If he did not, they would push him out by force.

The situation on the ground was getting worse and worse. By then, the head of the family—our children's grandfather—finally agreed to the idea of fleeing the country.

The men decided to leave with their families in the early hours of the following day. Everyone was thinking of what to take

Escaping the Invasion

with them. What would you take if you were forced to leave your home country?

Nothing!

There was no place to carry extra belongings in the cars. We had to leave everything and run for our lives.

Early the next day, the cars were crammed with people. Four cars were filled with men, women, and children. We left with no promise of ever returning to our homes.

The Amir of Kuwait at the United Nations

Iraqi tanks sit in the open desert, blocking the way

Chapter Six

The Ride Across the Desert

Off we went.

The sun was shining intensely. It was August, the hottest month of the year in Kuwait.

The plan was to take the main road to Saudi Arabia, the neighboring country to the south. It was a trip that would normally take only one hour. But this trip was like no other.

Every two miles there was a checkpoint with Iraqi soldiers. Their faces were stern as they inspected the fleeing cars. Further along, we saw all the cars in front of us change course into the desert.

The Iraqis had closed all the highways leading to the Kingdom of Saudi Arabia. There was no other way except across the vast open desert.

The caravan of cars followed a red pickup truck. It was driven by a Bedouin (Bedouins are people who lives in the desert) who was experienced and knew the terrain leading to safety. We had no choice but to follow him. Once the truck took the lead, the other cars tagged along into the soft sands of the Arabian Desert.

Escaping the Invasion

In the flat desert, many cars were stuck. It was very difficult to drive through the soft sand. We passed by some cars that were driven by women. They were fleeing with their children alone. Their husbands were captured by the Iraqis.

Many did not make it.

Many cars sank. One of these cars was my own car, a white 1984 Mazda. One of our friends with his family needed a car to escape. Like many other people, he left it there stuck in the sand. There was no time to dig it out under these circumstances.

Some families were trapped in the middle of nowhere, waiting for help that never came. Families left their stalled cars and wandered in the desert on foot. Many died of thirst and exposure.

The scene was horrifying. I looked at the people struggling on foot. I knew that I could have been in their situation.

In my lap, my son Abdullah was surprisingly calm. He had lost his liveliness and was growing weak. I took off his clothes and left him only in his thin, sleeveless, white cotton underwear. His tender face was turning reddish blue. His cheeks were saggy, and his eyes were half open.

I couldn't hear his lovely voice. I missed his giggles. He used to wake up around this time from his noon nap time with a shy, beautiful smile. For which I would sacrifice the whole world.

I rallied my strength. I was determined to live, to continue the wild trip to the end. I wanted my son to survive and be in this world. I yearned for my energy to pass through him and not to give up.

My husband was busy driving. He was very alert. In the past four years of our marriage, I knew him as a very kind-hearted, gentle, and caring man.

Today I came to see a fighter. He was focused on his mission to take us out of harm's way. He was like an Arabian knight, dressed all in white, who was determined to win his battle.

Heroically, he drove as fast as the desert simoom. (The simoom is the hot wind in the desert.) Incredibly, he was the only one of the whole caravan who controlled his car and didn't sink in the sand!

He didn't give this a chance to happen. Our car was soaring across the sand at a very swift speed. I was terrified as the car jumped up and down. I screamed out loud as the ride became frantic.

Kuwait is considered the hottest inhabited place on earth. The temperature neared 122 degrees Fahrenheit (50 degrees Celsius). For those who have never experienced the desert in the middle of the summer, it would be impossible to even imagine the deadly heat.

One car in our caravan hit the ground hard, and the radiator leaked. The car began to leak steam. The fumes came out the front of the car, and the car stopped. My brother-in-law, his wife, and his sister with her three children were stuck. The car was bogged down in the sand.

Escaping the Invasion

It was risky to bring our car to a complete stop in the sand because the wheels might sink into the ground. Despite the danger, we stopped to help them.

Clearly the car was overheated and needed water. But we only had drinking water! Without hesitating, my husband handed them our drinking water.

My brother-in-law quickly filled the radiator before the Iraqis could capture us. We waited for fifteen long minutes. Luckily, the car's wheels caught and pulled out of the sand. We set off again.

But in that time we had lost the Bedouin in the red pickup leading the caravan. He was the only man in the caravan who knew the desert. Along with the other cars, they had left us.

We still treasure our 1983 gold Mercedes!

Alone in the desert

Chapter Seven

Alone in the Desert

We were all alone in the vast desert. We didn't know where to go or which direction would lead us to safety.

The drivers of the four cars were my husband, my brother-in-law, my husband's sixty-five-year-old father, and my husband's uncle. His uncle was diabetic and carried his seventy-five-year-old blind mother in the front seat.

When I looked around, I saw pale faces, lost eyes, and desperate souls in need of shelter and security. There was not much talking. Silence prevailed, and the day seemed endless.

To make matters worse, I didn't know anything about my two sisters, whom I'd spoken to earlier that morning. I'd only learned that they'd left at about the same time.

I was very worried about them. But I kept it hushed in my heart. What could I do? I thought about them in these severe conditions. I felt hopeless.

We continued driving through the desert. It was midday by then, and the sun was directly overhead. The heat was intense. The sand was blistering.

Escaping the Invasion

Then on the horizon I saw two tanks facing each other, blocking the way. My heart was beating rapidly out of panic. "What do they want?" I thought.

"God help us," I prayed.

My brother-in-law stopped his car and talked to the Iraqi soldiers.

"Where are you going?" a fuming soldier clutching a machine gun asked him.

"We are leaving to—our ranch," he replied swiftly. They were the first words that came to his mind.

"We have orders. No one crosses the borders of Kuwait," one of the Iraqi soldiers barked out with a harsh voice.

"Go back!" he commanded.

In desperation, my brother-in-law pleaded with one of them. He asked him to let us pass for the sake of the children and the elderly who couldn't take it any longer. While he pleaded, we kept quiet. I prayed in my heart for a miracle.

Five minutes passed. We were afraid that they would turn us back, take us prisoners, or take our cars and leave us in the desert.

While I thought of the worst, I saw the cannons of the two tanks raise up high. One of the soldiers signaled with his hand to move.

It was a moment of triumph. We were set free. I couldn't believe the cars were truly moving by. I wanted time to speed up so we could be away from there as soon as possible. I wanted to be gone before they could change their minds.

Feeling relief mixed with uneasiness, we continued on our way to nowhere.

Cars stuck in the sand

Chapter Eight

Battling Death

As we headed south, our car was again soaring, barely touching the ground. The car was jumping up and down violently. I was terrified.

The caravan of cars kept moving until the inevitable occurred. One car stalled—the car of my husband's uncle. The old black Chevrolet wouldn't move an inch, even with everyone pushing and trying to dig it out of the sand.

Feeling the pinch of time, the sweaty and exhausted men decided to leave the car. We somehow made room for them in our three remaining vehicles.

His family moved quickly to join their cousins. While sitting in our car watching the chaos, I saw his tiny seventy-five-year-old blind mother. She was escorted by her son, stretching her hands out to the middle of the desert. She walked with half her legs covered with burning hot sand, trying to reach the other car. Watching her in such a dreadful condition broke my heart. I hid my head in my hands and wept.

We didn't think we would make it. The cars became heavier with more people. The extra weight made it harder to drive over the soft sand. Any car could easily sink. The journey became slower and more difficult. A long time had passed, and we didn't seem to be getting anywhere.

Amidst those tiring circumstances, I watched my son's face turned more reddish. His breaths became shorter and shallower. His seven tender months couldn't handle the heat and the long hours in the sweltering car. Holding him tight, I panicked, thinking, "My son is dying!"

Tears ran down my face as despair and dark thoughts overwhelmed me.

Then I suddenly remembered tossing a bag of oranges in the backseat earlier that morning. I urgently looked for the oranges and found them below. I took an orange in my hand and bit it in half. Then I squeezed the juice into my baby's mouth.

Moving his lips and tongue, he swallowed the sour squirt of the juice. He made faces and asked for more with a look of his eyes that demanded me to continue squeezing. Eventually, I could see that he slowly and steadily revived.

I was in such high spirits that I forgot for a moment that we were still in the middle of nowhere. My baby was alive again! I covered him with kisses. I laughed aloud and felt an emotional high only a mother could understand.

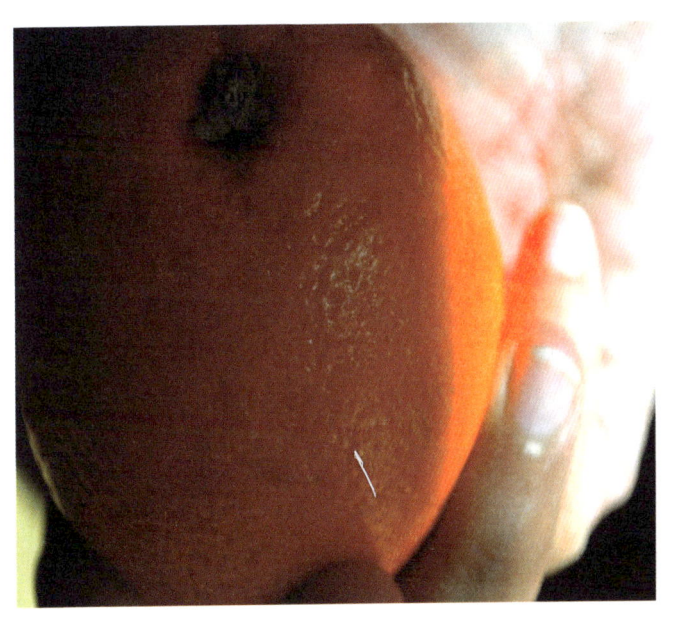

The orange that saved my son's life.

A low, grim building sits in the middle of the desert

Chapter Nine

The Reunion

For all of us, the challenge was great. The exodus was a never-ending ordeal. We fled our country fearful of being captured by Iraqi soldiers as we crossed the infinite sizzling desert in the caravan of cars. It was a merciless experience, facing death and the unknown.

At around three o'clock in the afternoon, the situation had not changed. Continuing our fast ride, I heard my husband at the lead scream, "There's a red pickup. Look!"

There was a car ahead, but who was it?

Was he a friend or foe?

The man in the red vehicle smiled and waved. I was happy, but cautious. I could not believe my eyes that there were other people around us again. Then the man gestured to follow him. We all turned to the east, deeper into the desert. In shock and exhausted, we couldn't react other than to wait and see what came next.

To our surprise, we came upon a ragged and dirty building in the middle of nowhere. As we approached, we could see many cars parked around it. Our pale faces shined with excitement. We all exchanged looks of joy. We hoped to have a drink of water or a place to rest.

I could see many escaped Kuwaitis and their vehicles. People were standing around talking. They all appeared very gloomy. I was still in a state of shock. I felt awkward. "Where are we?"

I still clung to my son. He seemed lifeless more than anything. As I got out of the car, suddenly someone grabbed my son from my arms. The man dashed with him inside the building. I screamed for my husband to help. We both ran after him.

The middle-aged man carrying my son was wearing a light beige fluffy thoub (Kuwaiti dress code). He reached the first room of the dimly lit hallway. I still couldn't see his face.

He turned towards the door and held my son up in his hands. He howled out, "Here's Abdullah! Abdullah is alive! He is here!"

We caught up with him inside the ghostly room. I was struck to see low-voiced weeping women and children crying. The room was completely empty except for people who were sitting on the pale ground. Among those teary, sad eyes, I came across two familiar faces. They were the faces of my two sisters!

I screamed their names and fell on the floor sobbing. We hugged and cried, thanking God for our safety. The man who took Abdullah was my sister's husband. He had also risked his life and saved his family who were visiting Kuwait. Earlier in

Cars at the Saudi boarders

the day, he was almost shot from behind when he refused to stop his car at the border of Saudi Arabia.

He told us how the Iraqi soldiers had commanded him to go back to the city. They fired at his car when he stepped on the gas with all his might to escape.

We rejoiced to see each other and exchanged our stories of how we made it so far. It was hard to believe what had happened. As we spoke, it felt like a movie, starting from making the decision to escape, leaving our homes and belongings, and crossing the desert with all the hardships that we faced. I could not soak up all that had occurred to us. I couldn't believe that we were finally safe.

Feeling more secure, we all got back into the cars and headed to Khafji, a Saudi town on the borders between Kuwait and Saudi Arabia. We were told that we were very close already.

We were also given cold water to drink by the Saudi guards stationed in the ragged building, which was a rest area for their army.

The hard part of the journey was over, but it would be another seven months of homelessness until Kuwait would be free again. With the help of the whole world and the determined Security Council of the United Nations, we were able to return and rebuild our lives.

The End

Map of Kuwait

Appendix

A Short History of Kuwait

Since ancient times, Kuwait has served as the gateway to the Middle East because of its geographical location. Kuwait has drawn upon the accumulated wisdom of countries around the world to power its own growth. In a few decades after the discovery of oil, a nation of fishermen and traders was transformed into one of the richest developed nations in the world. Kuwait now offers state-of-the-art amenities, a secure infrastructure with modern facilities and technical excellence, and is respected around the world.

The Kuwaitis' pride in their history, heritage, and national progress has given rise to an identity which is uniquely Kuwaiti. The centuries have changed; the traditions have not. The country has modernized, but its people's links with their heritage are as strong as ever. Kuwait's wealth—black gold—may be buried underground, but its spirit is still vibrantly free and alive.

LOCATION

Kuwait lies at the northwest corner of the Arabian Gulf, between 28° and 30° latitude and between 46° and 48° longitude. To the north and the west, it shares a border of 240 kilometers (149 miles) with the Republic of Iraq. To the south and southwest, it shares 250 kilometers (155 miles) with the Kingdom of Saudi Arabia. On the east, it has a coastline of 290 kilometers (181 miles) on the Arabian Gulf.

Copyright (c) 2007 By Huda Al-Medlej

The flag of Kuwait

Reader's Guide

Discussion Questions:

1- Why does Huda decide to turn her story into a book? Why do you think it is important to read about other people's stories of survival? Would you like to share your story of survival if you have been through one?

2- How would you answer the question of Chapter five? Would you stay or leave if your country is invaded, and your homes are intruded?

   Do you think leaving your country in such a situation is a good thing to do? Do you agree to the decision of Huda's family to leave?

3- If you were forced to leave your home or country, what would you take along with you?

4- Have you been in a desert before? Can you bear the heat of 122 degrees Fahrenheit (around 50 degrees Celsius)? Do a little experiment to feel this heat, and find out how long you can endure it.

5- Where is Kuwait located? And what is it famous for?

Huda M. Al-Medlej

About the Author

Huda Al-Medlej has always kept a diary ever since she was 16 years old in which she writes her daily thoughts and events. This has helped her in recalling the details of the story.

She has a bachelor of English Literature from Kuwait University 1986, and a Masters of Art in Education, TESOL(Teaching English to speakers of other languages) from New York University 2001.

In 1994 She moved with her husband who worked for the Kuwaiti Mission to the United Nations where they spent 14 years in New York City. She now lives in Madrid, Spain with her husband who works for Kuwait Embassy to Spain, with her four children and a cat. She is leading an active life where she practices her two passions, Reiki (Energy Healing) and life coaching.

She is a board member of The Arab Diplomatic Ladies' association in Madrid where she helps in building bridges between the two cultures.

You can contact Huda by email shahanyu@hotmail.com

Reviews of the book

Escaping the Invasion is a short and simple narrative of the author and her family's escape from Kuwait, beginning with the invasion and ending shortly thereafter at the Saudi border. It is intended for a teen reader, and would be a good way to personalize a history lesson with a brief personal story.

Osho.
Goodreads' librarian , the world's largest site for readers and book recommendations, USA

*

History is being fingerprinted by this personal experience of agony. The past can enrich our children's future, I truly recommend it for schools around the world.

Rihab Al-Medlej
Principle of intermediate School, Private Education and ex-English teacher. Kuwait

*

I truly enjoyed how this author captivated my imagination with her memories of the invasion of Kuwait. It was intriguing from beginning to end as she describes from her point of view (the toughest decision we had ever made). As an educator I recommend this quick reading as a reference to that invasion. This book is full of history and passion. The kind of passion that can only come from a mother telling her children of such an eventful, historical moment in her life.

Jacqueline Jones, YMCA educator. NEW YORK CITY.

This book is beautifully written.It's very deep and it's remarkable how a difficult situations make you do extraordinary things.A mother courage story that shows how difficult is to live and leave a country in war!!!

Stone Chick. Brazil

*

The best part of beginning my life here in Madrid is meeting a very admirable Kuwaiti woman, Huda Al-Medlej, who wrote a book called, «Escaping The Invasion», where she lies her tragic experience on small 59 pages that count up to limitless of feelings. A brave woman that aims to tell every Kuwaiti, especially teens who haven't been born by that time, on what happened and there's no shame or hurt in telling a truthful story. Thank you for making me live this little dark days with you. I really loved reading it.

MIM Student Haneen Al Rashid, I E University, Madrid

*

Escaping The Invasion touched our hearts through honesty, pure emotions and how the details were able to make us live the story . No matter how old a person is , every one would be greatfull to read it , and know the history of Kuwait, Best of luck!

Awaiting her next book !

Al Nayyerh reading group, Al jalees project,Kuwait

NOTE

NOTE

NOTE